Soul,
if by chance you forget where I am,
do not rush around here and there,
If you want to find me,
seek me inside yourself.

Soul,
you are my room,
you are my house, you are my dwelling.
If, through your distracted ways,
I ever find your door tightly closed,
do not seek me outside yourself.

To find me,
it will be enough simply to call me
and I will come quickly.
Seek me inside yourself.

St. Teresa of Avila

Copyright © 2019 Barbara Brownyard.
Barbarabrownyard.com

All rights reserved. No part of this book may be used or reproduced by any means, graphic, electronic, or mechanical, including photocopying, recording, taping or by any information storage retrieval system without the written permission of the author except in the case of brief quotations embodied in critical articles and reviews.

This book is a work of non-fiction. Unless otherwise noted, the author and the publisher make no explicit guarantees as to the accuracy of the information contained in this book and in some cases, names of people and places have been altered to protect their privacy.

WestBow Press books may be ordered through booksellers or by contacting:

WestBow Press
A Division of Thomas Nelson & Zondervan
1663 Liberty Drive
Bloomington, IN 47403
www.westbowpress.com
1 (866) 928-1240

Because of the dynamic nature of the Internet, any web addresses or links contained in this book may have changed since publication and may no longer be valid. The views expressed in this work are solely those of the author and do not necessarily reflect the views of the publisher, and the publisher hereby disclaims any responsibility for them.

Book Design:
Dawn Daisley, www.dawndaisleydesigns.com

ISBN: 978-1-9736-5000-3 (sc)
ISBN: 978-1-9736-5001-0 (e)

Library of Congress Control Number: 2018915175

Print information available on the last page.

WestBow Press rev. date: 1/9/2019

## Gratitude

Thank you always to my Divine Spirit God.

For my spiritual family,
who offer me unconditional love and support.

For Dawn Daisley,
who picked up all the pieces and made them look great.

My family,
whom I love with all my heart, especially my husband, Bruce.

# Sitting in the Silence

Barbara Brownyard

## Introduction

Welcome! I hope you will enjoy sitting down with these pictures – on a cozy bench – and slowly read the words that have emanated from my heart.

When I was in One Spirit Interfaith Seminary, one of my Deans said to me "Barbara, meditation will be your stretch". I was balking at the idea of sitting quietly for more than five minutes! It took me a while to begin. It came slowly, first using a guided meditation, then being able to sit for 2-3 minutes. It was hard. I had a million thoughts fly through my cluttered brain. They just didn't want to be silenced!

Practice, practice, practice – that's what I did. I struggled and fought. Then, one day, there it was- just a second of peace. The peace I sought all my life. And it was always there. I found that I just needed to surrender to that Voice within, without fighting it. It is all in the letting go-of ego, control, fear-all the things I thought were keeping me alive were really preventing me from growing in the Spirit.

Now meditating isn't so much of a struggle. It still takes some time to settle in and really feel present in the quiet.

I look forward to my time alone with the Divine, my Source of Love and Life. Some days can be glorious and others can come up dry. I know that Mother Teresa of Calcutta didn't hear from her Love for the years she gave of service but she kept at it, without wavering.

I've been collecting bench pictures for many years. They call me to rest. I can rest my weary soul, my busy mind and spend some time with the One who can heal me and replenish me. I always identified with Martha who was so busy in the kitchen while Jesus was teaching a new way of thinking to her sister Mary and their friends. This Martha has learned when to pay attention and listen for what is important.

May you find your own time to find that spark within and keep the flame of love alive. Your God is as close to you as your breath.

Love and Light,
Barbara

> Take a breath. You can do that.
> Be grateful; Enjoy it.
> Really let the air come in and
> feed every crevice of your body.
> Feel it feeding your very being,
> your life force.
>
> Then let it go, releasing it
> fully back to the world with
> peace and gratitude—
> Knowing another waits in the
> very next moment.

*AnnE O'Neil,* **If you Want the Rainbow, Welcome the Rain**

A sunny bench. What an inviting spot! The soft sounds of a waterfall trickles down below and the cool breeze caresses your cheeks.

Plop yourself down and sit with me. We'll talk, maybe sing, laugh, whisper, touch or just be together.

A bench just sits there and waits. It calls you to stop and relax. Sit and put your feet up — sit in the warm sunshine and heal.

How long can you sit?
Can you give the Divine a few minutes of your day? There are answers found in the sitting, on this wise old bench.

The side of the bench reads
"Feeding your senses nourishes your soul…"

This beautiful butterfly beckons me to nourish my soul by
sitting for a few minutes and taking in the beauty of this day,
this moment in time that I will never have again.

The smell of the fresh air that I inhale through my nostrils
nourishes my cells. The sun that touches my face as I look toward
the beautiful blue sky provides me with my vitamin D.

I hear the seagull "caw-caw" overhead and love how
he playfully swoops with the breezes.

My cells are pulsing with energy, life and gratitude as I sit.

I need the water to feed my soul.

Sitting at this beach, with a cup of joe early on Sunday mornings,
I start my week. I call this place "Bridge to Serenity."

As I look out on the beautiful ocean,
I know that Creator is fully in charge. Each cloud above my
head has been placed there. We are all accounted for.

He knows each drop of water in that body of water
and each grain of sand under my feet.

I am in awe of the majesty and humbled by how vast our Creator's love is for us.

Wow!

All the benches in the park are empty today.

I have my pick of where I want to sit and just BE. The sun is strong and I feel the warmth kissing my face. A slight breeze goes by and I hear the whisper of the Divine inviting me to "Just be still."

I treasure this time. It is so precious. It fills me with joy, with hope and strength. Just a few minutes alone with the Love Source within is delicious!

It has been a busy time.

Family, friends, meals, outdoor sports, lots of gatherings.
We had fun together but it is time for me to take some time alone.

This is when I re-group and recharge my battery again.
I know that balance is not easy. Rest and Recover.

Hang out with Spirit who knows just what I need when I need it.

So it is, when I sit and listen. I rest during my quiet time.
I leave filled with joy knowing that I have been loved and heard.

I can't wait for the next time of bliss.

This bench has been enveloped by the earth.

How many adults, children and animals have plopped
down in this spot over the years for a minute's rest?
If I sit for longer than a minute, will the ivy grow around me?

I am intrigued by the ivy's tenacity.
It doesn't care who it snuggles up to. It surrounds the bench
to make it just a bit more beautiful and inviting.

We humans can be that: bringing out the very best in each other,
by our words, our attentive listening or by a snuggle.

Waiting on this beautiful inviting bench.

Am I too underdressed to be sitting here? No, not me!
I am perfectly perfect, a beautiful reflection of the inner light I hold.
Do I dare relax, enjoying the beauty of the bench?

I know I am perfect in the eyes of the Divine.
That is the only one I need impress.

And guess what? No need to do that, either!!!!

> **Everything has its wonders, even darkness and silence, and I learn, whatever state I may be in, there in to be content.**

*Helen Keller*

A simple place to stop and wait. People watching is fun.
Where are they all running to and why? Spending a few
precious minutes doing nothing is foreign to me.

I "should" be doing this or that. Even when I am sitting,
I feel I should be doing something constructive, like doing
a crossword or solving the world's financial woes.

Today, I can sit, breathe, close my eyes and be in a state of nothingness.

No guilt, no shame, no need to make excuses.

Five little benches in the woods.
I rest after hiking, take one of the seats and laugh a little
to myself as I look around. Who placed these cute little
perfectly cut logs here? Who sat here before me?

Enough of the questions that probably really don't matter anyway.

It is a perfect little place to quietly sit and count all my blessings.
I smell the deep earthiness of the moss and feel sheltered by the
tall stately trees. The grass is so soft, I want to lie down and
roll around in it. I want to just breathe in and relish
all that nature has to offer my senses.

May I be always in wonder. May I always be grateful.

Have a rest, dear soul. Your heart is heavy.

Lay down your burdens with me. I don't have all the answers. I've been in your shoes, though, and will give you something that has no material value:

Time.

I have heard you sigh. It was a long, deep one. How have you been able to contain all that in your heart for so long?

I want to hear you, to see you and to be a safe place for you to relax your mind.

Be here. Be yourself. Be your truest self. I know you and hear you.

I still continue to question:
Who is God? Who am I? Am I part of God?
Where is God in all the mess?

It's easy to see God in beauty. Can God hear me?
Does God know my fears? If I tell my secrets, will they be heard?

I feel this bench calling to me. It has been hewn with loving hands.

The artist found the old driftwood and had the vision
to fashion a bench from it. How often do we pass something
beautiful and think "it's just an old piece of junk?"

Seeing something ordinary and creating something extraordinary.
That's me!

A lovely spot to take in the lake.

Who sat here before? Many travelers, I would imagine. Lovers meeting for a soft kiss. Hikers rest and have a sip of water.

The swans and ducks dive for a meal and mind their own business. There is a stream below.

The water's song as it makes its way down to the lake is a hymn from the Creator.

The fall is setting in with its glorious colors. Funny how the
leaves turn quicker when they are near a body of water.

I look forward to the cooler weather yet don't want to
face the bleak darkness the winter brings.

I always have struggled with darkness. Is it in my DNA?
I need to keep a balance during all the seasons. My attitude is key.

If I focus on the darkness, it permeates through me.
If I focus on the goodness and light shining within me, all is well.

I am always reminded that today is all we have.

Children playing in the surf.

Are they two friends taking their brothers out to test the water? Two sisters and their younger siblings? Their human chain is keeping them stable and safe as the waves come one by one.

We learned how to respect the ocean and trust that the waves will bring us back to safety on the shore. Sometimes, we take chances and try swimming alone. The tide pulls us away. We are warned to go with it and swim away from the trouble. Do I have enough faith to go with the urge to fight the monstrous sea?

With faith that we will be held up in the safe arms of our God, we let go and surrender.

> "We shall not cease from exploration
> And the end of all our exploring
> Will be to arrive where we started
> And know the place for the first time."
>
> *T. S. Eliot*

Thank you for giving me a sunny spot to sit and rest.

I bask in the warmth and listen for you. I close my eyes for a few minutes, relishing whispers of breezes that float by my waiting face.

I repeat again and again "Thank You." "You're welcome, dear child," you whisper back.

Can I be more content?
I know the love that has always been inside.

I am made of pure love, for I am made from YOU!

A huge old banyan tree. Sitting in its shade and thinking of all the roots that have extended out through the centuries.

How many have sat here and rested for a while? What has the tree observed? A mother sat with her baby and the tree extended its roots to her. An older man thought of his failing heart and the root went out to him, offering him solace. Young lovers snuck a kiss and the tree sighed.

The years gave it strength to be of service to the neighbors and visitors. Its roots extend and say "welcome."

Can you smell the softness in the air here?
Can you hear the birds as they dance over your head?
They swoop and dive,
enjoying the breezes that the inlet offers. I rest
and enjoy the fullness of nature today.

My heart is full with joy to have brought me to this place of rest.
I savor each minute, taking no heed of time.

This is bliss.

A peaceful spot to sit on a beautiful Fall day.

It is quiet and peaceful-just the squirrels scampering around the trees, happily chasing each other. I take a few deep breaths.

Ahhhh!
The world falls away as I just breathe in the good clean air. My lungs fill, my heart keeps beating and I melt into the seat. What more do I need? The bench holds me up as gravity keeps me down.

How magical it all seems. If I can take a minute to just be grateful for that, I know my Creator God smiles down upon me.

I feel very loved.

I love this sturdy bench that is available for walkers
to stop on their way into town.

I look at the vines winding up the side of the tree. "I am the vine, you are the branches." The branches extend to the sun and the rains nourish the roots from the ground, just like we are nourished and grounded by our sitting.

How can I get more of this blissful grace? I thrive as a spiritual being when I take the time to sit, to be grateful and remember.

A special place to sit and to BE.
This area holds a lot of local history. I think of the First
Nation people who fished and hunted on this land.

Do their spirits remain in the soil and the old trees? Who were they and what happened to their families? If I sit, will I hear their voices, asking me to remember them and the love they had for their land?

I am one with the earth and its beauty astounds me.

A quiet place in the sun to sit alone or with a friend and talk about the day.

Have I made a difference in someone's life
since I awoke this morning? Have I smiled, despite the ache
in my heart over the loss of a loved one or a painful phone call?

I know that, with the help of a power that is greater than puny
old me, I can change my attitude with a single thought.

My time sitting has given me a greater insight into who
runs the show. And it's certainly not me!

My meditation and prayer today are for those who sat
on this bench before me and made a difference in someone's life.

> **The universe is wired for God's light the way a house is wired for electricity, and every mind is like a lamp.**
>
> *Marianne Williamson, Tears to Triumph*

The innocence and simplicity of children!
I am in awe of their beautiful open smiles, trusting eyes
with the whole world open for them to experience.

My childhood wasn't perfect.
I made plenty of mistakes and probably didn't appreciate
my parents as much as I could. But they taught me love
of family and especially love for my God.

Those lessons have helped me every day of my life.

A little bench in a friend's garden.

I've passed by it often on the way to see her. Her garden gloves and spade are often left there, waiting for her return to this, her sangha.

The garden is small. It houses statuary symbolizing our stages of life: childhood, adolescence and adulthood.

I imagine her weeding and coming upon one that she ponders as the work progresses. She may sit for a bit in front of one that is resounding in her heart at that moment.

So it is with our sitting.
Waiting, listening, hoping for a word, smiling as it appears.

I love this spot on the lake to sit for a moment during my morning walk.

My still-beating heart appreciates the workout it's been given. I thank
my Creator-God for the ability to walk on my own two feet,
to breathe clean air, to be free to walk wherever I want
to go and the freedom to express myself.

Complacency fades as I continually focus on gratitude.

What an exquisite little settee! I found it on my
journey and take it home through my lens.

I have often seen my life as a mosaic.
The pieces have fallen together as I have grown.

Each piece represents a life experience. I am sure that some of
the tougher experiences have fortified the joyful or beautiful
ones that I see in the incomplete picture. Little did I know that,
through the pain, I would eventually appreciate the struggle.

And, so I continue to fill in the pieces of the puzzle.
It looks like it is going to be a beautiful story of a life well-lived!

These benches have probably seen a lot.

How many parents sat there with their little ones? Or maybe an older resident resting for a few hours after lunch, and then making their way home for an afternoon nap. The homeless have found this bench, too. Maybe for a night, before they are "asked" to move along.

My prayers go out to them, silent blessings for all.

I take my turn on this old bench, feeling a part of the "One" who knows and hears all our prayers.

My meditation as I sit is light.
My bench is set in a cute little park that is set up for
children to take their lunch or enjoy a snack.

I imagine the squeals of the children who first spy the animals
on the bench. I am reminded to have fun and play.

How often I tell myself that I need balance between work and play.
I shut my eyes, take a few deep breaths and offer a prayer of
gratitude for air to breathe and sun to warm my face.

Time for a swing, rest your head.
Look up at the sky and wonder.
Have you a few minutes for the Divine? Take a moment. Listen.
Feel your heartbeat. Catch the love!

See it – Feel it – Smell it.
All your senses are alive at this one moment.

> **In this quiet place inside, you naturally have access to your intuitive inner guidance. You could think of it as a wise part of you that lives in this deep place within you. It knows exactly what you need at every moment.**
>
> *Shaki Gawain, Developing Intuition*

My Beloved, I am tired and cranky.

I have had a lot of stress and haven't taken time to be alone to recharge my batteries. Help me to remember that You are my resting place. My source of comfort when the anxiety of just being a human gets to me. Sooth my anxious heart. I need You and sometimes forget that You are there for me, always.

I sit and give You some time. Then I know I can keep going.

Thank you, I leave my spot with a better attitude.

My backyard has a bench that has seen better days.

Yet, I have a hard time getting rid of it. It is moldy, warped and missing slats. Like me, it's not perfect but is ITSELF.

My bench has offered me several hours of sitting. The bird feeder and butterfly bush offer some company. If I am very still, I can fool them into thinking I am a statue!

I hone my senses as I listen, smell, feel and see the wonders from my own hometown bench.

So much sadness in the world today.

Sometimes, I just want to go up to the mess-makers and shout "Could you all please stop arguing!" It hurts my heart.

Maybe my sitting today will give me a time-out to pray for them. Can I even pray for me? My hope is that I will change and that will emanate into the world.

Just for today, I will offer my fellow human spirits a smile, a gesture that we are all one and that hope is just around the corner.

Sitting with a friend is the greatest gift.

Lovely flowers or trinkets are nice, but someone's whole attention is priceless. When I meet my friend on a bench, either at a park or in my backyard, we can be eye to eye.
I savor the quiet when neither one of us speaks.

It gives Spirit room to fill the space and lets us go deeper into our hearts. What more could my Divine Love ask of me?

How many souls need a hand to hold or an ear to listen. "Love one another as I have loved you." Yes, Beloved, yes.

Sometimes I feel that when I am practicing my sitting, the voices come through my head and then are filtered through my brain.

Then they come out of my mouth as I would interpret them, with all the filters and experiences that I've been through added to them.

Is this what you feel? Is there that inner critic inside you that keeps you from just seeing what the Divine wants you to see?

Maybe the truly enlightened ones have the knack of just hearing the Inner Voice at its purist, without all the sticky and messy pre-conceptions and histories they carry around with them.

They have learned to let go and be totally present, in the sublime presence.

What happened to me in my practice today was magical. Perhaps "miraculous" might be a better word to describe it.

All the fears and pains of my past were sent up in a cloud. I asked my Dear Beloved God to take care of them as I sat in the stillness.

It was as if a cool breeze came through my body.
I was free of the icky black crud that I carry around in my head.
I could be free to just bask in the light of Beloved's gaze
and enjoy the connection. When it was over,
I could take the cloud back or just leave it!

Who am I without that cloud? Do those experiences define me?
Am I bold and brave enough to live a life without them?

## About the Author

Barbara Brownyard is an Interfaith Minister and Certified Spiritual Counselor from the One Spirit Learning Alliance in New York City, N.Y.

She facilitates retreats and workshops for women and men. Her ministry also includes officiating at funerals, memorial services, gravesite services and baby blessings.

Her current passion is working with the Breakthrough Mercy Haven, Inc. program as a mentor and minister to formerly and currently homeless men and women.

She is a nationally published author and monthly columnist with various venues as well as on the world wide web. Find her work at Barbarabrownyard.com

CPSIA information can be obtained at www.ICGtesting.com
Printed in the USA
LVIW012131091120
671245LV00035B/146